George Orwell, Hanif Kureishi,
Zadie Smith

Cultural Encounters –

Three Stories Exploring the Colonial Legacy

Annotations by
Daniela Anton, Ellen Butzko
and Susanne Pongratz

Ernst Klett Sprachen
Stuttgart

Bildquellennachweis:
5 picture alliance/AP Photo; **17** GARY DOAK / Alamy Stock Foto;
33 agefotostock (AGF/Mimmo Frassineti), Barcelona

1. Auflage 1 ^{13 12 11 10 9} | 2026 25 24 23 22

Titel der Originalausgaben
Shooting an Elephant, Copyright © George Orwell. First published in
New Writing, 1936.
My Son the Fanatic, Copyright © Hanif Kureishi. First published in
The New Yorker, 1994.
The Embassy of Cambodia, Copyright © Zadie Smith. First published in
The New Yorker, 2013
© Ernst Klett Sprachen GmbH, Rotebühlstraße 77, 70178 Stuttgart 2020
Alle Rechte vorbehalten.
www.klett-sprachen.de

Herausgegeben von Dr. Daniela Anton
Worterklärungen von Dr. Daniela Anton *(The Embassy of Cambodia)*,
Ellen Butzko und Susanne Pongratz *(My Son the Fanatic* und *Shooting
an Elephant)*

Redaktion: Debby Böhm und Astrid Proctor
Gestaltung und Satz: Joachim Schrimm, Friolzheim
Umschlaggestaltung: Eva Lettenmayer
Titelbild: Getty Images (tomgigabite), München; Shutterstock
(stockphoto-graf), New York; Shutterstock (Nattan J), New York;
Getty Images (FOTOKITA), München
Druck und Bindung: CPI books GmbH, Leck

Printed in Germany
ISBN 978-3-12-579386-6

9 783125 793866

Contents

Abbreviations used in the annotations

BE	British English	*opp of*	opposite of
e.g.	for example	*os*	oneself
esp	especially	*pl*	plural
fig	figurative	*sb*	somebody
fml	formal	*sl*	slang (be careful
inf	informal		how you use it)
Lat	Latin	*sth*	something
neg	negative	*vulg*	vulgar
old	old-fashioned language		

George Orwell

Biographical note

George Orwell was born Eric Arthur Blair in 1903 in India. His paternal grandfather served in the Indian Army under the British Raj (= British rule in India before 1947) and his father worked in the Indian Civil Service. Later Orwell described his family as belonging to the "lower-upper middle class" and indeed his parents owed their privileged lifestyle to the British Empire.

Blair returned to England in 1907 with his mother and sister. He won a scholarship to Eton, the famous English public school, where he developed a strong dislike of the English class system.

Blair failed to win a university scholarship and he joined the Indian Imperial Police in 1922. He served in the police force in Burma for five years and, like many colleagues, had a native mistress. In 1927 he resigned, having come to feel like the "hand of the oppressor" through his support of imperialism, a political system he had grown to resent.

As a result of his experiences, Blair wrote *Burmese Days* (1934). Its central character Flory, a timber merchant (= sb who sells wood) in Burma, eventually commits suicide because he feels alienated from both his fellow colonialists and the Burmese natives. He hates the corruption among English and Burmese officials, and the white Europeans' arrogance towards the natives.

In 1928, Blair decided to live among the poor of London and Paris for a time. He regarded them – like the Burmese – as victims of injustice. He described his experiences in his auto-biographical *Down and Out in Paris and London* (1933). Blair also changed his name to George Orwell: Eric Blair suited an Etonian and colonial policeman, so he became George Orwell, classless and anti-authoritarian (George is an ordinary English name, the Orwell is a river in East Anglia).

In 1936, still under the influence of Burma, he wrote the essay, "Shooting an Elephant". It later served as the title of a collection of essays dealing with a wide range of topics.

At the end of 1936 Orwell fought on the Republican side in the Spanish Civil War, because he was fascinated by the vision of a democratic society without class distinctions. He returned from the war wounded and disillusioned, having realized that – just as in Burma – there would always be something in human nature that wants power over others.

In 1938, Orwell fell ill with tuberculosis and never really recovered. In 1945, he wrote *Animal Farm*, a political satire about a society where all animals are equal, but "some are more equal than others". *Nineteen Eighty-four*, a utopian novel about an oppressive society that uses torture to make its citizens love the government, another variation on the theme of "man's dominion over man", was published in 1949.

George Orwell died in January 1950.

GEORGE ORWELL

Shooting an Elephant

In Moulmein, in Lower Burma, I was hated by large numbers
of people – the only time in my life that I have been important
enough for this to happen to me. I was sub-divisional police
officer of the town, and in an aimless, petty kind of way anti-
5   European feeling was very bitter. No one had the guts to raise
a riot, but if a European woman went through the bazaars
alone somebody would probably spit betel juice over her dress.
As a police officer I was an obvious target and was baited
whenever it seemed safe to do so. When a nimble Burman
10 tripped me up on the football field and the referee (another
Burman) looked the other way, the crowd yelled with hideous
laughter. This happened more than once. In the end the
sneering yellow faces of young men that met me everywhere,
the insults hooted after me when I was at a safe distance, got
15 badly on my nerves. The young Buddhist priests were the worst
of all. There were several thousands of them in the town and
none of them seemed to have anything to do except stand on
street corners and jeer at Europeans.
    All this was perplexing and upsetting. For at that time I had
20 already made up my mind that imperialism was an evil thing
and the sooner I chucked up my job and got out of it the better.
Theoretically – and secretly, of course – I was all for the
Burmese and all against their oppressors, the British. As for
the job I was doing, I hated it more bitterly than I can perhaps

---

4 **petty** narrow-minded – 5 **guts** *(inf)* courage – 7 **betel juice red** liquid produced by
chewing betel nuts (= *Betelnuss)* – 8 **to bait sb** to make cruel remarks to make sb
angry, to tease sb – 9 **nimble** agile, swift, quick in one's movements – 10 **referee** person
who makes sure that players follow the rules – 11 **hideous** horrible – 13 **sneering**
laughing in an unkind way – 14 **to hoot** *here:* to cry loudly to show one's disapproval –
18 **to jeer** to shout rudely and laugh – 21 **to chuck sth up** *(inf)* to give sth up –
23 **oppressor** sb who rules using force

make clear. In a job like that you see the dirty work of Empire at close quarters. The wretched prisoners huddling in the stinking cages of the lock-ups, the grey, cowed faces of the long-term convicts, the scarred buttocks of the men who had
5 been flogged with bamboos – all these oppressed me with an intolerable sense of guilt. But I could get nothing into perspective. I was young and ill-educated and I had had to think out my problems in the utter silence that is imposed on every Englishman in the East. I did not even know that the
10 British Empire is dying, still less did I know that it is a great deal better than the younger empires that are going to supplant it. All I knew was that I was stuck between my hatred of the empire I served and my rage against the evil-spirited little beasts who tried to make my job impossible. With one part of
15 my mind I thought of the British Raj as an unbreakable tyranny, as something clamped down, *in saecula saeculorum*, upon the will of prostrate peoples; with another part I thought that the greatest joy in the world would be to drive a bayonet into a Buddhist priest's guts. Feelings like these are the normal by-
20 products of imperialism; ask any Anglo-Indian official, if you can catch him off duty.

One day something happened which in a roundabout way was enlightening. It was a tiny incident in itself, but it gave me a better glimpse than I had had before of the real nature
25 of imperialism – the real motives for which despotic govern- ments act. Early one morning the sub-inspector at a police station the other end of the town rang me up on the phone and said that an elephant was ravaging the bazaar. Would I

---

2 **at close quarters from** nearby – 2 **wretched** miserable – 2 **to huddle** to be in a big group in a small space – 3 **cowed** afraid – 4 **convict** prisoner – 4 **scarred** marked by wounds which have healed – 4 **buttock** part of the body one sits on – 5 **to flog** to beat severely – 5 **to oppress sb** *here:* to make sb feel unhappy – 8 **to impose sth on sb** to force sb to accept sth – 11 **to supplant** *(fml)* to replace – 15 **British Raj** British rule in India between 1858 and 1947 – 16 **to clamp down** *here:* to rule by force – 16 *in saecula saeculorum (Lat)* for ever – 17 **prostrate** *(here fig)* lying face down on the ground – 18 **bayonet** long knife which can be fixed on the end of a rifle *(Flinte)* – 22 **roundabout** indirect – 24 **glimpse** a short look – 28 **to ravage** to destroy

please come and do something about it? I did not know what I could do, but I wanted to see what was happening and I got on to a pony and started out. I took my rifle, an old 44 Winchester and much too small to kill an elephant, but I
5 thought the noise might be useful *in terrorem*. Various Burmans stopped me on the way and told me about the elephant's doings. It was not, of course, a wild elephant, but a tame one which had gone 'must'. It had been chained up as tame elephants always are when their attack of 'must' is due,
10 but on the previous night it had broken its chain and escaped. Its mahout, the only person who could manage it when it was in that state, had set out in pursuit, but he had taken the wrong direction and was now twelve hours' journey away, and in the morning the elephant had suddenly reappeared in the town.
15 The Burmese population had no weapons and were quite helpless against it. It had already destroyed somebody's bamboo hut, killed a cow and raided some fruit-stalls and devoured the stock; also it had met the municipal rubbish van, and, when the driver jumped out and took to his heels, had
20 turned the van over and inflicted violence upon it.

The Burmese sub-inspector and some Indian constables were waiting for me in the quarter where the elephant had been seen. It was a very poor quarter, a labyrinth of squalid bamboo huts, thatched with palm-leaf, winding all over a steep
25 hillside. I remember that it was a cloudy stuffy morning at the beginning of the rains. We began questioning the people as to where the elephant had gone and, as usual, failed to get any definite information. That is invariably the case in the East; a story always sounds clear enough at a distance, but the nearer
30 you get to the scene of events the vaguer it becomes. Some of

---

5 *in terrorem (Lat)* as a warning – 8 **to go 'must' (of elephants)** to be in sexual heat and go out of control – 11 **mahout** *(India)* person who trains and works with an elephant – 17 **to raid** to carry out an attack – 18 **to devour** to eat hungrily – 18 **municipal** referring to a town – 19 **to take to one's heels** to run away – 20 **to inflict violence** *here:* to attack and damage – 21 **constable** *(BE)* regular police officer – 23 **squalid** dirty, poor – 24 **thatched** having a roof of dried grass – 25 **stuffy** when there is no air movement – 28 **invariably** always

the people said that the elephant had gone in one direction, some said that he had gone in another, some professed not even to have heard of any elephant. I had almost made up my mind that the whole story was a pack of lies, when we heard
5　yells a little distance away. There was a loud, scandalized cry of "Go away, child! Go away this instant!" and an old woman with a switch in her hand came round the corner of a hut, violently shooing away a crowd of naked children. Some more women followed, clicking their tongues and exclaiming;
10　evidently there was something there that the children ought not to have seen. I rounded the hut and saw a man's dead body sprawling in the mud. He was an Indian, a black Dravidian coolie, almost naked, and he could not have been dead many minutes. The people said that the elephant had
15　come suddenly upon him round the corner of the hut, caught him with its trunk, put its foot on his back and ground him into the earth. This was the rainy season and the ground was soft, and his face had scored a trench a foot deep and a couple of yards long. He was lying on his belly with arms crucified
20　and head sharply twisted to one side. His face was coated with mud, the eyes wide open, the teeth bared and grinning with an expression of unendurable agony. (Never tell me, by the way, that the dead look peaceful. Most of the corpses I have seen looked devilish.) The friction of the great beast's foot had
25　stripped the skin from his back as neatly as one skins a rabbit. As soon as I saw the dead man I sent an orderly to a friend's house nearby to borrow an elephant rifle. I had already sent

2 **to profess sth** to claim sth which may not be true – 5 **scandalized** horrified – 7 **switch** thin, flexible stick – 8 **to shoo sb away** to chase sb away *esp* by waving one's arms – 12 **to sprawl** to lie untidily – 13 **Dravidian** belonging to one of the aboriginal races of India – 13 **coolie** worker with no particular training – 16 **trunk** *Rüssel* – 16 **to grind, ground, ground** to press down with force – 18 **to score a trench** to cut a channel – 19 **yard** distance equal to 0.9144 metres – 19 **crucified** *here:* with arms stretched out as if nailed to a cross – 21 **to bare** to show – 22 **unendurable** hard to bear – 22 **agony** great suffering – 24 **friction** rubbing one thing against another – 26 **orderly** an officer's assistant

back the pony, not wanting it to go mad with fright and throw me if it smelled the elephant.

The orderly came back in a few minutes with a rifle and five cartridges, and meanwhile some Burmans had arrived and
5 told us that the elephant was in the paddy fields below, only a few hundred yards away. As I started forward practically the whole population of the quarter flocked out of the houses and followed me. They had seen the rifle and were all shouting excitedly that I was going to shoot the elephant. They had not
10 shown much interest in the elephant when he was merely ravaging their homes, but it was different now that he was going to be shot. It was a bit of fun to them, as it would be to an English crowd; besides, they wanted the meat. It made me vaguely uneasy. I had no intention of shooting the elephant –
15 I had merely sent for the rifle to defend myself if necessary – and it is always unnerving to have a crowd following you. I marched down the hill, looking and feeling a fool, with the rifle over my shoulder and an ever-growing army of people jostling at my heels. At the bottom when you got away from
20 the huts there was a metalled road and beyond that a miry waste of paddy fields a thousand yards across, not yet ploughed but soggy from the first rains and dotted with coarse grass. The elephant was standing eighty yards from the road, his left side towards us. He took not the slightest notice of the crowd's
25 approach. He was tearing up bunches of grass, beating them against his knees to clean them and stuffing them into his mouth.

I had halted on the road. As soon as I saw the elephant I knew with perfect certainty that I ought not to shoot him. It
30 is a serious matter to shoot a working elephant – it is com-

---

4 **cartridge** unit of ammunition – 5 **paddy field** field in which rice is grown – 7 **to flock** to move in large groups – 11 **to ravage** to damage badly – 16 **unnerving** upsetting – 19 **to jostle** to push others in a group – 19 **at sb's heels** close behind sb – 20 **miry** muddy – 21 **ploughed** dug up ready for planting – 22 **soggy** soft, wet – 22 **dotted with sth** with sth randomly spread across an area – 22 **coarse** strong, rough

parable to destroying a huge and costly piece of machinery – and obviously one ought not to do it if it can possibly be avoided. And at that distance, peacefully eating, the elephant looked no more dangerous than a cow. I thought then and I
5 think now that his attack of 'must' was already passing off; in which case he would merely wander harmlessly about until the mahout came back and caught him. Moreover, I did not in the least want to shoot him. I decided that I would watch him for a little while to make sure that he did not turn savage
10 again, and then go home.

But at that moment I glanced round at the crowd that had followed me. It was an immense crowd, two thousand at the least and growing every minute. It blocked the road for a long distance on either side. I looked at the sea of yellow faces
15 above the garish clothes – faces all happy and excited over this bit of fun, all certain that the elephant was going to be shot. They were watching me as they would watch a conjurer about to perform a trick. They did not like me, but with the magical rifle in my hands I was momentarily worth watching. And
20 suddenly I realized that I should have to shoot the elephant after all. The people expected it of me and I had got to do it; I could feel their two thousand wills pressing me forward, irresistibly. And it was at this moment, as I stood there with the rifle in my hands, that I first grasped the hollowness, the
25 futility of the white man's dominion in the East. Here was I, the white man with his gun, standing in front of the unarmed native crowd – seemingly the leading actor of the piece; but in reality I was only an absurd puppet pushed to and fro by the will of those yellow faces behind. I perceived in this
30 moment that when the white man turns tyrant it is his own freedom that he destroys. He becomes a sort of hollow, posing

---

9 **savage** aggressive – 15 **garish** too bright in colour – 17 **conjurer** magician – 24 **to grasp** *here:* to understand – 24 **hollowness** worthlessness – 25 **futility** uselessness – 25 **dominion** rule – 28 **to and fro** backwards and forwards – 29 **to perceive sth** *(fml)* to become aware of sth – 31 **posing** trying to impress others

dummy, the conventionalized figure of a sahib. For it is the condition of his rule that he shall spend his life in trying to impress the 'natives' and so in every crisis he has got to do what the 'natives' expect of him. He wears a mask, and his
5 face grows to fit it. I had got to shoot the elephant. I had committed myself to doing it when I sent for the rifle. A sahib has got to act like a sahib; he has got to appear resolute, to know his own mind and do definite things. To come all that way, rifle in hand, with two thousand people marching at my
10 heels, and then to trail feebly away, having done nothing – no, that was impossible. The crowd would laugh at me. And my whole life, every white man's life in the East, was one long struggle not to be laughed at.

But I did not want to shoot the elephant. I watched him
15 beating his bunch of grass against his knees, with that preoccupied grandmotherly air that elephants have. It seemed to me that it would be murder to shoot him. At that age I was not squeamish about killing animals, but I had never shot an elephant and never wanted to. (Somehow it always seems
20 worse to kill a large animal.) Besides, there was the beast's owner to be considered. Alive, the elephant was worth at least a hundred pounds; dead, he would only be worth the value of his tusks – five pounds, possibly. But I had got to act quickly. I turned to some experienced-looking Burmans who had been
25 there when we arrived, and asked them how the elephant had been behaving. They all said the same thing: he took no notice of you if you left him alone, but he might charge if you went too close to him.

It was perfectly clear to me what I ought to do. I ought to
30 walk up to within, say, twenty-five yards of the elephant and test his behaviour. If he charged I could shoot, if he took no

---

1 **sahib** *(colonial India)* form of address used for a European male, master – 10 **to trail feebly** to walk weakly – 16 **preoccupied** thinking deeply – 18 **not to be squeamish about sth** not to be upset by sth unpleasant – 23 **tusk** long, pointed, bone-like tooth of an elephant – 27 **to charge** to run forward in order to attack

notice of me it would be safe to leave him until the mahout came back. But also I knew that I was going to do no such thing. I was a poor shot with a rifle and the ground was soft mud into which one would sink at every step. If the elephant
5 charged and I missed him, I should have about as much chance as a toad under a steam-roller. But even then I was not thinking particularly of my own skin, only of the watchful yellow faces behind. For at that moment, with the crowd watching me, I was not afraid in the ordinary sense, as I would have been if
10 I had been alone. A white man mustn't be frightened in front of 'natives'; and so, in general, he isn't frightened. The sole thought in my mind was that if anything went wrong those two thousand Burmans would see me pursued, caught, trampled on and reduced to a grinning corpse like that Indian
15 up the hill. And if that happened it was quite probable that some of them would laugh. That would never do. There was only one alternative. I shoved the cartridges into the magazine and lay down on the road to get a better aim.

The crowd grew very still, and a deep, low, happy sigh, as of
20 people who see the theatre curtain go up at last, breathed from innumerable throats. They were going to have their bit of fun after all. The rifle was a beautiful German thing with cross-hair sights. I did not then know that in shooting an elephant one should shoot to cut an imaginary bar running from ear-hole
25 to ear-hole. I ought therefore, as the elephant was sideways on, to have aimed straight at his ear-hole; actually I aimed several inches in front of this, thinking the brain would be further forward.

When I pulled the trigger I did not hear the bang or feel the
30 kick – one never does when a shot goes home – but I heard the devilish roar of glee that went up from the crowd. In that

6 **toad** *Kröte* – 6 **steam-roller** vehicle with large wheels which flattens road surfaces – 11 **sole** only – 17 **to shove** to push with force – 17 **magazine** part of a gun for the ammunition – 22 **cross-hair sights** aiming device – 24 **bar** *here:* line – 29 **trigger** device which is pulled back to fire a bullet – 31 **glee** happiness

instant, in too short a time, one would have thought, even for the bullet to get there, a mysterious, terrible change had come over the elephant. He neither stirred nor fell, but every line of his body had altered. He looked suddenly stricken, shrunken,
5 immensely old, as though the frightful impact of the bullet had paralysed him without knocking him down. At last, after what seemed a long time – it might have been five seconds, I dare say – he sagged flabbily to his knees. His mouth slobbered. An enormous senility seemed to have settled upon
10 him. One could have imagined him thousands of years old. I fired again into the same spot. At the second shot he did not collapse but climbed with desperate slowness to his feet and stood weakly upright, with legs sagging and head drooping. I fired a third time. That was the shot that did for him. You could
15 see the agony of it jolt his whole body and knock the last remnant of strength from his legs. But in falling he seemed for a moment to rise, for as his hind legs collapsed beneath him he seemed to tower upwards like a huge rock toppling, his trunk reaching skyward like a tree. He trumpeted, for the
20 first and only time. And then down he came, his belly towards me, with a crash that seemed to shake the ground even where I lay.

I got up. The Burmans were already racing past me across the mud. It was obvious that the elephant would never rise
25 again, but he was not dead. He was breathing very rhythmically with long rattling gasps, his great mound of a side painfully rising and falling. His mouth was wide open – I could see far down into caverns of pale pink throat. I waited a long

---

3 **to stir** to move a little – 4 **to alter** to change – 4 **stricken** suffering greatly –
4 **shrunken** having decreased in size –6 **to paralyse** *lähmen* – 8 **to sag** to fall heavily
– 8 **flabbily** loosely – 9 **to slobber** to let liquid fall from one's mouth – 13 **to droop** to
hang downwards – 14 **to do for sb** to kill sb – 15 **to jolt** to shake violently – 18 **to
topple** to fall – 26 **rattling** making a number of sounds – 26 **gasp** quick, deep breath –
26 **mound** a big heap – 28 **cavern** a large cave

time for him to die, but his breathing did not weaken. Finally I fired my two remaining shots into the spot where I thought his heart must be. The thick blood welled out of him like red velvet, but still he did not die. His body did not even jerk when
5 the shots hit him, the tortured breathing continued without a pause. He was dying, very slowly and in great agony, but in some world remote from me where not even a bullet could damage him further. I felt that I had got to put an end to that dreadful noise. It seemed dreadful to see the great beast lying
10 there, powerless to move and yet powerless to die, and not even to be able to finish him. I sent back for my small rifle and poured shot after shot into his heart and down his throat. They seemed to make no impression. The tortured gasps continued as steadily as the ticking of a clock.

15 In the end I could not stand it any longer and went away. I heard later that it took him half an hour to die. Burmans were arriving with dashs and baskets even before I left, and I was told they had stripped his body almost to the bones by the afternoon.

20 Afterwards, of course, there were endless discussions about the shooting of the elephant. The owner was furious, but he was only an Indian and could do nothing. Besides, legally I had done the right thing, for a mad elephant has to be killed, like a mad dog, if its owner fails to control it. Among the
25 Europeans opinion was divided. The older men said I was right, the younger men said it was a damn shame to shoot an elephant for killing a coolie, because an elephant was worth more than any damn Coringhee coolie. And afterwards I was very glad that the coolie had been killed; it put me legally in
30 the right and it gave me a sufficient pretext for shooting the elephant. I often wondered whether any of the others grasped that I had done it solely to avoid looking a fool.

Autumn, 1936

3 **to well** to flow – 4 **velvet** *Samt* – 4 **to jerk** to make a sudden movement –
7 **remote** far away – 12 **to pour** *here:* to fire – 17 **dash** *here probably* a variation of
Burmese **dha** or **dah** a type of knife – 28 **Coringhee** sb from Coringa in India –
30 **pretext** excuse for doing sth one should not do

Hanif Kureishi

Biographical note

Hanif Kureishi was born in Bromley, a London suburb, in 1954 to a Pakistani father and a white English mother. As the only Asian at school he experienced first-hand what it meant to be discriminated against as he was beaten up by classmates.

Indeed, much of his writing focuses on what it means to be the product of an interracial marriage. After studying philosophy and then supporting himself by writing pornographic stories under a pseudonym, Kureishi began his literary career as a playwright. His early plays were staged at theatres in London.

Kureishi gained a larger audience with his film screenplay *My Beautiful Laundrette* (1985) which won him several awards including an Oscar nomination. A British TV channel had asked Kureishi to write a screenplay about Pakistani immigrants in Britain. He set the film in London in the 1980s and explored issues that were to reappear in his fiction: homosexuality, racially mixed relationships and identities. Kureishi does not simply paint a black-and-white picture of racial stereotypes, he also critically reflects the immigrants' behaviour: "There isn't such a thing as an essential Asian experience any more than there is any other essential experience. Nobody's life can be reduced in that way." Thus Pakistanis were quite disturbed by *My Beautiful Laundrette* as it shows ambitious, middle-class Pakistanis who are not only homosexual but also ready to exploit whites. Other films which Kureishi wrote the screenplay for and directed include *Sammy and Rosie Get Laid* (1987) and *London Kills Me* (1991). His first novel, *The Buddha of Suburbia* (1990), was turned into a BBC TV-series (1993), and like his novel *The Black Album* (1995), features a young, second-generation Pakistani immigrant.

The short story "My Son the Fanatic" (1994) was made into a film in 1997. It is set in Bradford, an English town with a large Muslim population where Salman Rushdie's novel *The Satanic Verses* was burned in 1989. The film script differs from the short story in that it adds characters (Parvez's Islam-oriented wife and the white Fingerhut family whose daughter is engaged to Parvez's son at one point) and scenes (Parvez's son's involvement with the fundamentalist movement and Parvez's affair with the prostitute Bettina).

HANIF KUREISHI

My Son the Fanatic

Surreptitiously, the father began going into his son's bedroom. He would sit there for hours, rousing himself only to seek clues. What bewildered him was that Ali was getting tidier. The room, which was usually a tangle of clothes, books, cricket
5   bats and video games, was becoming neat and ordered: spaces began appearing where before there had been only mess.

Initially, Parvez had been pleased: his son was outgrowing his teenage attitudes. But one day, beside the dustbin, Parvez found a torn shopping bag that contained not only old toys
10 but computer disks, videotapes, new books, and fashionable clothes the boy had bought a few months before. Also without explanation, Ali had parted from the English girlfriend who used to come around to the house. His old friends stopped ringing.

15 For reasons he didn't himself understand, Parvez was unable to bring up the subject of Ali's unusual behaviour. He was aware that he had become slightly afraid of his son, who, between his silences, was developing a sharp tongue. One remark Parvez did make – "You don't play your guitar anymore"
20 – elicited the mysterious but conclusive reply, "There are more important things to be done."

Yet Parvez felt his son's eccentricity as an injustice. He had always been aware of the pitfalls that other men's sons had stumbled into in England. It was for Ali that Parvez worked
25 long hours; he spent a lot of money paying for Ali's education as an accountant. He had bought Ali good suits, all the books

Hanif Kureishi [həˈnɪːf kʊˈrɔɪʃi] – 1 **surreptitiously** secretly – 2 **to rouse os** to move, to stir – 3 **to bewilder** to confuse – 4 **tangle** confused mass of things – 9 **torn** full of holes – 20 **to elicit** to provoke – 20 **conclusive** final, convincing – 23 **pitfall** dangerous situation – 24 **to stumble** *here:* to get into difficulty by chance – 26 **accountant** person who controls the financial accounts of businesses he required, and a computer. And now the boy was throwing his possessions out! The TV, video-player and stereo system followed the guitar. Soon the room was practically bare. Even the unhappy walls bore pale marks where Ali's pictures had been removed.

Parvez couldn't sleep; he went more often to the whisky bottle, even when he was at work. He realised it was imperative to discuss the matter with someone sympathetic.

Parvez had been a taxi-driver for twenty years. Half that time he'd worked for the same firm. Like him, most of the other drivers were Punjabis. They preferred to work at night, when the roads were clearer and the money better. They slept during the day, avoiding their wives. They led almost a boy's life together in the cabbies' office, playing cards and setting up practical jokes, exchanging lewd stories, eating takeaways from local *balti* houses, and discussing politics and their own problems.

But Parvez had been unable to discuss the subject of Ali with his friends. He was too ashamed. And he was afraid, too, that they would blame him for the wrong turning his boy had taken just as he had blamed other fathers whose sons began running around with bad girls, skipping school and joining gangs.

For years, Parvez had boasted to the other men about how Ali excelled in cricket, swimming and football, and what an attentive scholar he was, getting As in most subjects. Was it asking too much for Ali to get a good job, marry the right girl, and start a family? Once this happened, Parvez would be happy. His dreams of doing well in England would have come true. Where had he gone wrong?

3 **bare** empty – 4 **to bear a mark (bore, born)** to show the signs of sth – 7 **imperative** extremely important 11 **Punjabi** sb from the province of Punjab, Pakistan – 14 **cabby** *(inf)* taxi-driver, from BE cab = taxi – 15 **lewd** vulgar, sexual – 16 *balti* spicy Indian dish served in a wok-like pot – 24 **to boast** to talk proudly about one's achievements – 25 **to excel** to do extremely well – 26 **scholar** student

One night, sitting in the taxi office on busted chairs with his two closest friends, watching a Sylvester Stallone film, Parvez broke his silence.

"I can't understand it!" he burst out. "Everything is going
5 from his room. And I can't talk to him any more. We were not father and son – we were brothers! Where has he gone? Why is he torturing me?" And Parvez put his head in his hands.

Even as he poured out his account, the men shook their heads and gave one another knowing glances.
10 "Tell me what is happening!" he demanded.

The reply was almost triumphant. They had guessed something was going wrong. Now it was clear: Ali was taking drugs and selling his possessions to pay for them. That was why his bedroom was being emptied.
15 "What must I do, then?"

Parvez's friends instructed him to watch Ali scrupulously and to be severe with him, before the boy went mad, overdosed, or murdered someone.

Parvez staggered out into the early-morning air, terrified
20 that they were right. His boy – the drug-addict killer!

To his relief, he found Bettina sitting in his car.

Usually the last customers of the night were local "brasses", or prostitutes. The taxi-drivers knew them well and often drove them to liaisons. At the end of the girls' night, the men would
25 ferry them home, though sometimes they would join the cabbies for a drinking session in the office. Occasionally, the drivers would go with the girls. "A ride in exchange for a ride," it was called.

Bettina had known Parvez for three years. She lived outside
30 the town and, on the long drives home, during which she sat not in the passenger seat but beside him, Parvez had talked

---

1 **busted** *(inf)* broken – 4 **to burst out (burst, burst)** to speak loudly, suddenly –
7 **to torture sb** to cause sb extreme pain – 8 **to pour sth out** *here:* to tell sth
eagerly – 8 **account** report – 16 **scrupulously** very carefully – 17 **severe** strict –
19 **to stagger** to walk unsteadily as if one is going to fall – 24 **liaison** *here:* meeting
place and/or person you are having a (secret) sexual relationship with – 27 **ride** *(double
meaning)* to give sb a lift in one's car/to have sex with sb

to her about his life and hopes, just as she talked about hers. They saw each other most nights.

He could talk to her about things he'd never be able to discuss with his own wife. Bettina, in turn, always reported on
5 her night's activities. He liked to know where she had been and with whom. Once, he had rescued her from a violent client, and since then they had come to care for each other.

Though Bettina had never met Ali, she heard about the boy continually. That night, when Parvez told Bettina that he
10 suspected Ali was on drugs, to Parvez's relief, she judged neither him nor the boy, but said, "It's all in the eyes." They might be bloodshot; the pupils might be dilated; Ali might look tired. He could be liable to sweats, or sudden mood changes. "OK?"

15 Parvez began his vigil gratefully. Now that he knew what the problem might be, he felt better. And surely, he figured, things couldn't have gone too far?

He watched each mouthful the boy took. He sat beside him at every opportunity and looked into his eyes. When he could,
20 he took the boy's hand, checked his temperature. If the boy wasn't at home, Parvez was active, looking under the carpet, in Ali's drawers, and behind the empty wardrobe – sniffing, inspecting, probing. He knew what to look for: Bettina had drawn pictures of capsules, syringes, pills, powders, rocks.

25 Every night, she waited to hear news of what he'd witnessed. After a few days of constant observation, Parvez was able to report that although the boy had given up sports, he seemed healthy. His eyes were clear. He didn't – as Parvez expected he might – flinch guiltily from his father's gaze. In fact, the boy
30 seemed more alert and steady than usual: as well as being sullen, he was very watchful. He returned his father's long

---

12 **bloodshot** red as if filled with blood – 12 **dilated** bigger than normal – 13 **to be liable to sth** *(fml)* to be likely to have sth – 15 **vigil** a purposeful watch – 16 **to figure** to think – 23 **to probe** to examine – 24 **syringe** tube with a needle for injections – 24 **rock** *(sl)* crack cocaine – 29 **to flinch** to make a sudden movement to avoid sth, to shy away from – 29 **gaze** a fixed look – 30 **alert** paying full attention – 31 **sullen** unwilling to talk

looks with more than a hint of criticism, of reproach, even – so much so that Parvez began to feel that it was he who was in the wrong, and not the boy.

"And there's nothing else physically different?" Bettina asked.

5 "No!" Parvez thought for a moment. "But he is growing a beard."

One night, after sitting with Bettina in an all-night coffee shop, Parvez came home particularly late. Reluctantly, he and Bettina had abandoned the drug theory, for Parvez had found

10 nothing resembling any drug in Ali's room. Besides, Ali wasn't selling his belongings. He threw them out, gave them away, or donated them to charity shops.

Standing in the hall, Parvez heard the boy's alarm clock go off. Parvez hurried into his bedroom, where his wife, still

15 awake, was sewing in bed. He ordered her to sit down and keep quiet, though she had neither stood up nor said a word. As she watched him curiously, he observed his son through the crack of the door.

The boy went into the bathroom to wash. When he returned

20 to his room, Parvez sprang across the hall and set his ear to Ali's door. A muttering sound came from within. Parvez was puzzled but relieved.

Once this clue had been established, Parvez watched him at other times. The boy was praying. Without fail, when he was

25 at home, he prayed five times a day.

Parvez had grown up in Lahore, where all young boys had been taught the Koran. To stop Parvez from falling asleep while he studied, the *maulvi* had attached a piece of string to the ceiling and tied it to Parvez's hair, so if his head fell forward,

30 he would instantly jerk awake. After this indignity, Parvez had avoided all religions. Not that the other taxi-drivers had any

---

1 **reproach** criticism – 8 **reluctantly** unwillingly – 9 **to abandon** to give up – 12 **charity shop** second-hand shop – 18 **crack** narrow opening – 21 **muttering** speaking very quietly – 22 **puzzled** confused – 24 **without fail** always – 26 **Lahore** capital of the province of Punjab in north-east Pakistan – 28 *maulvi* Muslim religious teacher – 30 **to jerk awake** to wake up suddenly – 30 **indignity** injury to one's self-respect

more respect than he. In fact, they made jokes about the local mullahs walking around with their caps and beards, thinking they could tell people how to live while their eyes roved over the boys and girls in their care.

5　　Parvez described to Bettina what he had discovered. He informed the men in the taxi office. His friends, who had been so inquisitive before, now became oddly silent. They could hardly condemn the boy for his devotions.

Parvez decided to take a night off and go out with the boy. 10　They could talk things over. He wanted to hear how things were going at college; he wanted to tell him stories about their family in Pakistan. More than anything, he yearned to understand how Ali had discovered the "spiritual dimension", as Bettina called it.

15　　To Parvez's surprise, the boy refused to accompany him. He claimed he had an appointment. Parvez had to insist that no appointment could be more important than that of a son with his father.

The next day, Parvez went immediately to the street corner 20　where Bettina stood in the rain wearing high heels, a short skirt, and a long mac, which she would open hopefully at passing cars.

"Get in, get in!" he said.

They drove out across the moors and parked at the spot 25　where, on better days, their view unimpeded for miles except by wild deer and horses, they'd lie back, with their eyes half-closed, saying, "This is the life." This time Parvez was trembling. Bettina put her arms around him.

"What's happened?"

30　　"I've just had the worst experience of my life."

---

3 **to rove** to look with the aim of starting a sexual relationship – 7 **inquisitive** curious – 8 **devotions** prayers, dedication – 12 **to yearn** to have a strong desire – 21 **mac** *short for* **mackintosh** raincoat – 25 **unimpeded** unrestricted – 28 **to tremble** to shake due to cold or fear

As Bettina rubbed his head Parvez told her that the previous evening, as he and his son had studied the menu, the waiter, whom Parvez knew, brought him his usual whisky-and-water. Parvez was so nervous he had even prepared a question. He was going to ask Ali if he was worried about his imminent exams. But first he loosened his tie, crunched a poppadum, and took a long drink.

Before Parvez could speak, Ali made a face.

"Don't you know it's wrong to drink alcohol?" he had said.

"He spoke to me very harshly," Parvez said to Bettina.

"I was about to castigate the boy for being insolent, but I managed to control myself."

Parvez had explained patiently that for years he had worked more than ten hours a day, had few enjoyments or hobbies, and never gone on holiday. Surely it wasn't a crime to have a drink when he wanted one?

"But it is forbidden," the boy said.

Parvez shrugged. "I know."

"And so is gambling, isn't it?"

"Yes. But surely we are only human?"

Each time Parvez took a drink, the boy winced, or made some kind of fastidious face. This made Parvez drink more quickly. The waiter, wanting to please his friend, brought another glass of whisky. Parvez knew he was getting drunk, but he couldn't stop himself. Ali had a horrible look, full of disgust and censure. It was as if he hated his father.

Halfway through the meal, Parvez suddenly lost his temper and threw a plate on the floor. He felt like ripping the cloth from the table, but the waiters and other customers were staring at him. Yet he wouldn't stand for his own son's telling him the difference between right and wrong. He knew he

---

5 **imminent** certain to happen soon – 6 **to crunch** to chew noisily – 6 **poppadum** thin, round, crisp Indian bread – 11 **to castigate** *(fml)* to criticize severely – 11 **insolent** rude, disrespectful – 18 **to shrug** to move your shoulders up and down to show that you don't care – 19 **gambling** playing games for money – 21 **to wince** to tighten your facial muscles suddenly as if in pain – 22 **fastidious** *here:* very critical – 26 **disgust** a strong dislike – 28 **to rip** to pull violently – 30 **to stand for sth** *(inf)* to allow sth to happen

wasn't a bad man. He had a conscience. There were a few things of which he was ashamed, but on the whole he had lived a decent life.

"When have I had time to be wicked?" he asked Ali.

5 In a low, monotonous voice, the boy explained that Parvez had not, in fact, lived a good life. He had broken countless rules of the Koran.

"For instance?" Parvez demanded.

Ali didn't need to think. As if he had been waiting for this 10 moment, he asked his father if he didn't relish pork pies?

"Well." Parvez couldn't deny that he loved crispy bacon smothered with mushrooms and mustard and sandwiched between slices of fried bread. In fact, he ate this for breakfast every morning.

15 Ali then reminded Parvez that he had ordered his wife to cook pork sausages, saying to her. "You're not in the village now. This is England. We have to fit in."

Parvez was so annoyed and perplexed by this attack that he called for more drink.

20 "The problem is this," the boy said. He leaned across the table. For the first time that night, his eyes were alive. "You are too implicated in Western civilisation."

Parvez burped; he thought he was going to choke. "Implicated!" he said. "But we live here!"

25 "The Western materialists hate us," Ali said. "Papa, how can you love something which hates you?"

"What is the answer, then," Parvez said miserably, "according to you?"

Ali didn't need to think. He addressed his father fluently, as 30 if Parvez were a rowdy crowd which had to be quelled or convinced. The law of Islam would rule the world; the skin of the infidel would burn off again and again; the Jews and

---

3 **decent** respectable – 4 **wicked** evil – 10 **to relish** to enjoy a lot – 12 **to smother** to cover thickly – 22 **implicated** involved – 23 **to burp** *rülpsen* – 23 **to choke** to not be able to breathe because sth is blocking your throat – 30 **rowdy** noisy, likely to cause trouble – 30 **to quell** to beat down – 32 **infidel** sb without religious beliefs

Christers would be routed. The West was a sink of hypocrites, adulterers, homosexuals, drug users and prostitutes.

While Ali talked, Parvez looked out the window as if to check that they were still in London.

5   "My people have taken enough. If the persecution doesn't stop, there will be *jihad*. I, and millions of others, will gladly give our lives for the cause."

"But why, why?" Parvez said.

"For us, the reward will be in Paradise."

10   "Paradise!"

Finally, as Parvez's eyes filled with tears, the boy urged him to mend his ways.

"But how would that be possible?" Parvez asked.

"Pray," urged Ali. "Pray beside me."

15   Parvez paid the bill and ushered his boy out of there as soon as he was able. He couldn't take any more.

Ali sounded as if he'd swallowed someone else's voice.

On the way home, the boy sat in the back of the taxi, as if he were a customer. "What has made you like this?" Parvez
20   asked him, afraid that somehow he was to blame for all this. "Is there a particular event which has influenced you?"

"Living in this country."

"But I love England," Parvez said, watching his boy in the rear view mirror. "They let you do almost anything here."

25   "That is the problem," Ali replied.

For the first time in years, Parvez couldn't see straight. He knocked the side of the car against a lorry, ripping off the wing mirror. They were lucky not to have been stopped by the police: Parvez would have lost his licence and his job.

30   Back at the house, as he got out of the car, Parvez stumbled and fell in the road, scraping his hands and ripping his

---

1 **Christer** *(slang)* Christian – 1 **to rout** to defeat completely – 1 **sink** *here:* a place where evil collects – 1 **hypocrite** sb who pretends to be what he/she is not – 2 **adulterer** sb who is sexually disloyal to a wife or husband – 6 *jihad* holy war by Muslims against non-Muslims in defence of the Islamic faith – 11 **to urge** to make a great effort to persuade – 12 **to mend one's ways** to improve morally – 15 **to usher** to lead – 30 **to stumble** to stagger, to almost fall down – 31 **to scrape** to injure through contact with sth rough

trousers. He managed to haul himself up. The boy didn't even offer him his hand.

Parvez told Bettina he was willing to pray, if that was what the boy wanted – if it would dislodge the pitiless look from
5 his eyes. "But what I object to," he said, "is being told by my own son that I am going to Hell!"

What had finished Parvez off was the boy's saying he was giving up his studies in accounting. When Parvez had asked why, Ali said sarcastically that it was obvious. "Western
10 education cultivates an anti-religious attitude."

And in the world of accountants it was usual to meet women, drink alcohol, and practise usury.

"But it's well-paid work," Parvez argued. "For years you've been preparing!"
15 Ali said he was going to begin to work in prisons, with poor Muslims who were struggling to maintain their purity in the face of corruption. Finally, at the end of the evening, as Ali went up to bed, he had asked his father why he didn't have a beard, or at least a moustache.
20 "I feel as if I've lost my son," Parvez told Bettina. "I can't bear to be looked at as if I'm a criminal. I've decided what to do."

"What is it?"

"I'm going to tell him to pick up his prayer mat and get out
25 of my house. It will be the hardest thing I've ever done, but tonight I'm going to do it."

"But you mustn't give up on him," said Bettina. "Many young people fall into cults and superstitious groups. It doesn't mean they'll always feel the same way." She said Parvez had to stick
30 by his boy.

---

1 **to haul os up** to pull os to one's feet with great effort – 4 **to dislodge** to remove –
12 **usury** *(fml, old)* lending money at an exorbitant rate of interest – 28 **superstitious** believing in things that are not real, e.g. magic – 29 **to stick by sb** to continue to try to help sb

Parvez was persuaded that she was right, even though he didn't feel like giving his son more love when he had hardly been thanked for all he had already given.

For the next two weeks, Parvez tried to endure his son's looks
5   and reproaches. He attempted to make conversation about Ali's beliefs. But if Parvez ventured any criticism, Ali always had a brusque reply. On one occasion, Ali accused Parvez of "grovelling" to the whites; in contrast, he explained, he himself was not "inferior"; there was more to the world than the West,
10 though the West always thought it was best.

"How is it you know that?" Parvez said. "Seeing as you've never left England?"

Ali replied with a look of contempt.

One night, having ensured there was no alcohol on his
15 breath, Parvez sat down at the kitchen table with Ali. He hoped Ali would compliment him on the beard he was growing, but Ali didn't appear to notice it.

The previous day, Parvez had been telling Bettina that he thought people in the West sometimes felt inwardly empty
20 and that people needed a philosophy to live by.

"Yes," Bettina had said. "That's the answer. You must tell him what your philosophy of life is. Then he will understand that there are other beliefs."

After some fatiguing consideration, Parvez was ready to
25 begin. The boy watched him as if he expected nothing. Haltingly, Parvez said that people had to treat one another with respect, particularly children their parents. This did seem, for a moment, to affect the boy. Heartened, Parvez continued. In his view, this life was all there was, and when you died, you
30 rotted in the earth. "Grass and flowers will grow out of my grave, but something of me will live on."

---

4 **to endure** to tolerate – 5 **reproach** criticism, dislike – 6 **to venture** to dare (to say sth) – 8 **to grovel** *(neg)* to behave in an excessively polite way – 13 **contempt** dislike – 24 **fatiguing** tiring – 26 **haltingly** uncertainly, slowly – 28 **to hearten** to encourage

Hanif Kureishi

"How then?"

"In other people. For instance, I will continue – in you."

At this the boy appeared a little distressed.

"And in your grandchildren." Parvez added for good measure.
5 "But while I am here on earth I want to make the best of it. And I want you to, as well!"

"What d'you mean by 'make the best of it'?" asked the boy.

"Well," said Parvez. "For a start … you should enjoy yourself. Yes. Enjoy yourself without hurting others."
10 Ali said enjoyment was "a bottomless pit".

"But I don't mean enjoyment like that," said Parvez. "I mean the beauty of living."

"All over the world our people are oppressed," was the boy's reply.
15 "I know," Parvez answered, not entirely sure who "our people" were. "But still – life is for living!"

Ali said, "Real morality has existed for hundreds of years. Around the world millions and millions of people share my beliefs. Are you saying you are right and they are all wrong?"
20 And Ali looked at his father with such aggressive confidence that Parvez would say no more.

A few evenings later, Bettina was riding in Parvez's car after visiting a client when they passed a boy on the street.

"That's my son," Parvez said, his face set hard. They were
25 on the other side of town, in a poor district, where there were two mosques.

Bettina turned to see. "Slow down, then, slow down!"

She said. "He's good-looking. Reminds me of you. But with a more determined face. Please, can't we stop?"

---

3 **distressed** upset – 4 **for good measure** to add an extra example – 10 **a bottomless pit** *here:* sth that uses up one's energy, sth dangerous and immoral – 26 **mosque** *Moschee*

"What for?"

"I'd like to talk to him."

Parvez turned the cab round and pulled up beside the boy. "Coming home?" Parvez asked. "It's quite a way."

5 The boy shrugged and got into the back seat. Bettina sat in the front. Parvez became aware of Bettina's short skirt, her gaudy rings and ice-blue eyeshadow. He became conscious that the smell of her perfume, which he loved, filled the cab. He opened the window.

10 While Parvez drove as fast as he could, Bettina said gently to Ali, "Where have you been?"

"The mosque," he said.

"And how are you getting on at college? Are you working hard?"

15 "Who are you to ask me these questions?" Ali said, looking out of the window. Then they hit bad traffic, and the car came to a standstill.

By now, Bettina had inadvertently laid her hand on Parvez's shoulder. She said, "Your father, who is a good man, is very 20 worried about you. You know he loves you more than his own life."

"You say he loves me," the boy said.

"Yes!" said Bettina.

"Then why is he letting a woman like you touch him like 25 that?"

If Bettina looked at the boy in anger, he looked back at her with cold fury.

She said, "What kind of woman am I that I should deserve to be spoken to like that?"

30 "You know what kind," he said. Then he turned to his father. "Now let me out."

"Never," Parvez replied.

---

7 **gaudy** colourful in a vulgar way – 18 **inadvertently** unintentionally – 27 **fury** uncontrolled anger

"Don't worry, I'm getting out," Bettina said.

"No, don't!" said Parvez. But even as the car moved forward, she opened the door and threw herself out – she had done this before – and ran away across the road. Parvez stopped
5 and shouted after her several times, but she had gone.

Parvez took Ali back to the house, saying nothing more to him.

Ali went straight to his room. Parvez was unable to read the paper, watch television, or even sit down. He kept pouring
10 himself drinks.

At last, he went upstairs and paced up and down outside Ali's room. When, finally, he opened the door, Ali was praying. The boy didn't even glance his way.

Parvez kicked him over. Then he dragged the boy up by the
15 front of his shirt and hit him. The boy fell back. Parvez hit him again. The boy's face was bloody. Parvez was panting; he knew the boy was unreachable, but he struck him none the less. The boy neither covered himself nor retaliated: there was no fear in his eyes. He only said, through his split lip. "So who's the
20 fanatic now?"

11 **to pace** to walk back and forth nervously – 13 **to glance** to look quickly – 16 **to pant** to breathe noisily – 18 **to retaliate** to hit back when sb hurts you

Zadie Smith

Biographical note

Sadie Adeline Smith was born in 1975 in Willesden in the north-west London borough of Brent, which is also where "The Embassy of Cambodia" is set.

Her mother, Yvonne Bailey from Jamaica, was thirty years younger than Sadie's English father, Harvey Smith, and they eventually got divorced when Sadie was a teenager. At the age of 14, Sadie also changed her name to Zadie.

Zadie Smith studied literature at Cambridge University's King's College and published a number of short stories while still a student. She also found herself a literary agent and submitted part of her début novel *White Teeth*. This was auctioned to publishers before it was even completed, and – once published – became an immediate and widely acclaimed best-seller and won several awards and prizes. Smith has written a number of other successful novels and many short stories and essays, both fiction and non-fiction. Her writing frequently covers themes of race and postcolonial identity as well as religion. She has not only been shortlisted (and longlisted) for various awards, but has won several of them, for example the *Whitbread First Novel Award, Commonwealth Writers' Best Book Award* and the *Langston Hughes Medal*, to name but a few.

Smith worked as a writer-in-residence at the Institute of Contemporary Art (ICA) in London, was a Fellow of the Radcliffe Institute for Advanced Study at Harvard University, taught fiction at the Columbia University School of Arts and since 2010 is a tenured professor of fiction at New York University. She is considered one of the twenty most influential people in British culture.

Zadie Smith and her husband Nick Laird, whom she met at Cambridge University, have two children and are based in New York City and Queen's Park, London.

ZADIE SMITH

The Embassy of Cambodia

0–1

Who would expect the Embassy of Cambodia? Nobody. Nobody could have expected it, or be expecting it. It's a surprise, to us all. The Embassy of Cambodia!
5 Next door to the embassy is a health centre. On the other side, a row of private residences, most of them belonging to wealthy Arabs (or so we, the people of Willesden, contend). They have Corinthian pillars on either side of their front doors, and – it's widely believed – swimming pools out back. The
10 embassy, by contrast, is not very grand. It is only a four- or five-bedroom North London suburban villa, built at some point in the thirties, surrounded by a red brick wall, about eight feet high. And back and forth, cresting this wall horizontally, flies a shuttlecock. They are playing badminton in the Embassy of
15 Cambodia. Pock, smash. Pock, smash.
  The only real sign that the embassy is an embassy at all is the little brass plaque on the door (which reads, "THE EMBASSY OF CAMBODIA") and the national flag of Cambodia (we assume that's what it is – what else could it be?) flying
20 from the red tiled roof. Some say, "Oh, but it has a high wall around it, and this is what signifies that it is not a private residence, like the other houses on the street but, rather, an embassy." The people who say so are foolish. Many of the private houses have high walls, quite as high as the Embassy
25 of Cambodia's – but they are not embassies.

2 **embassy** building in which government officials representing their government in a foreign country work – 7 **Willesden** an area in north-west London – 8 **Corinthian pillars** tall, decorative structure in the style of the old city of Corinth in Greece – 13 **to crest** to rise up to a peak before falling again – 14 **shuttlecock** the object that you hit over the net when playing badminton – 17 **brass** a yellow shiny metal made from zinc and copper

0–2

On the sixth of August, Fatou walked past the embassy for the first time, on her way to a swimming pool. It is a large pool, although not quite Olympic size. To swim a mile you must
5   complete eighty-two lengths, which, in its very tedium, often feels as much a mental exercise as a physical one. The water is kept unusually warm, to please the majority of people who patronize the health centre, the kind who come not so much to swim as to lounge poolside or rest their bodies in the sauna.
10 Fatou has swum here five or six times now, and she is often the youngest person in the pool by several decades. Generally, the clientele are white, or else South Asian or from the Middle East, but now and then Fatou finds herself in the water with fellow-Africans. When she spots these big men, paddling
15 frantically like babies, struggling simply to stay afloat, she prides herself on her own abilities, having taught herself to swim, several years earlier, at the Carib Beach Resort, in Accra. Not in the hotel pool – no employees were allowed in the pool. No, she learned by struggling through the rough gray sea, on
20 the other side of the resort walls. Rising and sinking, rising and sinking, on the dirty foam. No tourist ever stepped onto the beach (it was covered with trash), much less into the cold and treacherous sea. Nor did any of the other chambermaids. Only some reckless teenage boys, late at night, and Fatou, early
25 in the morning. There is almost no way to compare swimming at Carib Beach and swimming in the health centre, warm as it is, tranquil as a bath. And, as Fatou passes the Embassy of Cambodia, on her way to the pool, over the high wall she sees a shuttlecock, passed back and forth between two unseen
30 players. The shuttlecock floats in a wide arc softly rightward, and is smashed back, and this happens again and again, the

5 **tedium** monotony, boredom – 8 **to patronize** to visit, to use – 12 **clientele** [ˌkliːɑ̃ˈtel] customers – 15 **frantically** wildly, desperately – 17 **Accra** capital city of Ghana – 23 **treacherous** dangerous – 23 **chambermaid** a woman who cleans and tidies rooms in a hotel – 27 **tranquil** calm, peaceful

first player always somehow able to retrieve the smash and transform it, once more, into a gentle, floating arc. High above, the sun tries to force its way through a cloud ceiling, gray and filled with water. Pock, smash. Pock, smash.

5 **0–3**

When the Embassy of Cambodia first appeared in our midst, a few years ago, some of us said, "Well, if we were poets perhaps we could have written some sort of an ode about this surprising appearance of the embassy." (For embassies are 10 usually to be found in the centre of the city. This was the first one we had seen in the suburbs.) But we are not really a poetic people. We are from Willesden. Our minds tend toward the prosaic. I doubt there is a man or woman among us, for example, who – upon passing the Embassy of Cambodia for 15 the first time – did not immediately think: "genocide."

0–4

Pock, smash. Pock, smash. This summer we watched the Olympics, becoming well attuned to grunting, and to the many other human sounds associated with effort and the triumph 20 of the will. But the players in the garden of the Embassy of Cambodia are silent. (We can't say for sure that it is a garden – we have a limited view over the wall. It may well be a paved area, reserved for badminton.) The only sign that a game of badminton is under way at all is the motion of the shuttlecock

---

13 **prosaic** [prə(ʊ)ˈzeɪɪk] lacking imagination or originality – 15 **genocide** massacre of a people. In Cambodia, 1.5 to 2 million people (about a quarter of the population) were persecuted and killed between 1975 and 1979 by the Khmer Rouge, a totalitarian Communist regime, whose aim was to forcefully turn Cambodia into a socialist agrarian republic. – 18 **attuned to** accustomed to, able to recognize

itself, alternately being lobbed and smashed, lobbed and smashed, and always at the hour that Fatou passes on her way to the health centre to swim (just after ten in the morning on Mondays). It should be explained that it is Fatou's employers
5   – and not Fatou – who are the true members of this health club; they have no idea that she uses their guest passes in this way. (Mr and Mrs Derawal and their three children – aged seventeen, fifteen, and ten – live on the same street as the embassy, but the road is almost a mile long, with the embassy
10 at one end and the Derawals at the other.) Fatou's deception is possible only because on Mondays Mr Derawal drives to Eltham to visit his mini-market there, and Mrs Derawal works the counter in the family's second mini-mart, in Kensal Rise. In the slim drawer of a faux-Louis XVI console, in the entrance
15 hall of the Derawals' primary residence, one can find a stockpile of guest passes. Nobody besides Fatou seems to remember that they are there.

Since August 6th (the first occasion on which she noticed the badminton), Fatou has made a point of pausing by the
20 bus stop opposite the embassy for five or ten minutes before she goes in to swim, idle minutes she can hardly afford (Mrs Derawal returns to the house at lunchtime) and yet seems unable to forgo. Such is the strangely compelling aura of the embassy. Usually, Fatou gains nothing from this waiting and
25 observing, but on a few occasions she has seen people arrive at the embassy and watched as they are buzzed through the gate. Young white people carrying rucksacks. Often they are scruffy, and wearing sandals, despite the cool weather. None of the visitors so far have been visibly Cambodian. These
30 young people are likely looking for visas. They are buzzed in

---

1 **to lob** to hit sth high into the air so that it flies in a curve – 10 **deception** the act of deceiving sb/of hiding sth – 14 **faux-Louis XVI console** a piece of furniture (a kind of cabinet) built in an antique style but actually just a replica – 21 **idle** unproductive, not doing anything – 23 **to forgo** to give up – 23 **compelling** very interesting or exciting – 28 **scruffy** untidy, dirty

and then pass through the gate, although Fatou would really have to stand on top of the bus stop to get a view of whoever it is that lets them in. What she can say with certainty is that these occasional arrivals have absolutely no effect on the
5 badminton, which continues in its steady pattern, first gentle, then fast, first soft and high, then hard and low.

0–5

On the twentieth of August, long after the Olympians had returned to their respective countries, Fatou noticed that a
10 basketball hoop had appeared in the far corner of the garden, its net of synthetic white rope rising high enough to be seen over the wall. But no basketball was ever played – at least not when Fatou was passing. The following week it had been moved closer to Fatou's side of the wall. (It must be a mobile
15 hoop, on casters.) Fatou waited a week, two weeks, but still no basketball game replaced the badminton, which carried on as before.

0–6

When I say that we were surprised by the appearance of the
20 Embassy of Cambodia, I don't mean to suggest that the embassy is in any way unique in its peculiarity. In fact, this long, wide street is notable for a number of curious buildings, in the context of which the Embassy of Cambodia does not seem especially strange. There is a mansion called
25 GARYLAND, with something else in Arabic engraved below GARYLAND, and both the English and the Arabic text are inlaid in pink-and-green marble pillars that bookend a gigantic

---

15 **casters** a set of wheels – 21 **peculiarity** unusualness – 24 **mansion** a large house, villa – 27 **to bookend** to be positioned at the end of sth

fence, far higher than the embassy's, better suited to a fortress. Dramatic golden gates open automatically to let vehicles in and out. At any one time, GARYLAND has five to seven cars parked in its driveway.

5 There is a house with a huge pink elephant on the doorstep, apparently made of mosaic tiles.

There is a Catholic nunnery with a single red Ford Focus parked in front. There is a Sikh institute. There is a faux-Tudor house with a pool that Mickey Rooney rented for a season, 10 while he was performing in the West End fifteen summers ago. That house sits opposite a dingy retirement home, where one sometimes sees distressed souls, barely covered by their dressing gowns, standing on their tiny balconies, staring into the tops of the chestnut trees.

15 So we are hardly strangers to curious buildings, here in Willesden & Brondesbury. And yet still we find the Embassy of Cambodia a little surprising. It is not the right sort of surprise, somehow.

0–7

20 In a discarded Metro found on the floor of the Derawal kitchen, Fatou read with interest a story about a Sudanese "slave" living in a rich man's house in London. It was not the first time that Fatou had wondered if she herself was a slave, but this story, brief as it was, confirmed in her own mind that she was not. 25 After all, it was her father, and not a kidnapper, who had taken her from Ivory Coast to Ghana, and when they reached Accra they had both found employment in the same hotel. Two years later, when she was eighteen, it was her father again who had

---

7 **nunnery** convent for women – 8 **faux** not real, fake – 8 **Tudor** built in the style used during the reign of the Tudor dynasty in Britain (1485–1603) – 9 **Mickey Rooney** (1920–2014) American film star – 11 **dingy** dark, gloomy, depressing – 12 **distressed** troubled, upset, miserable – 20 **Metro** a free newspaper which is distributed on trains and buses and in other public spaces in the UK

organized her difficult passage to Libya and then on to Italy
– a not insignificant financial sacrifice on his part. Also, Fatou
could read English – and speak a little Italian – and this girl
in the paper could not read or speak anything except the
5   language of her tribe. And nobody beat Fatou, although Mrs
Derawal had twice slapped her in the face, and the two older
children spoke to her with no respect at all and thanked her
for nothing. (Sometimes she heard her name used as a term
of abuse between them. "You're as black as Fatou." Or "You're
10 as stupid as Fatou.") On the other hand, just like the girl in
the newspaper, she had not seen her passport with her own
eyes since she arrived at the Derawals', and she had been told
from the start that her wages were to be retained by the
Derawals to pay for the food and water and heat she would
15 require during her stay, as well as to cover the rent for the
room she slept in. In the final analysis, however, Fatou was
not confined to the house. She had an Oyster Card, given to
her by the Derawals, and was trusted to do the food shopping
and other outside tasks for which she was given cash and told
20 to return with change and receipts for everything. If she did
not go out in the evenings that was only because she had no
money with which to go out, and anyway knew very few people
in London. Whereas the girl in the paper was not allowed to
leave her employers' premises, not ever – she was a prisoner.
25 On Sunday mornings, for example, Fatou regularly left the
house to meet her church friend Andrew Okonkwo at the 98
bus stop and go with him to worship at the Sacred Heart of
Jesus, just off the Kilburn High Road. Afterward Andrew always
took her to a Tunisian café, where they had coffee and cake,
30 which Andrew, who worked as a night guard in the City, always
paid for. And on Mondays Fatou swam. In very warm water,

---

2 **sacrifice** the act of giving up sth valuable in order to gain sth else or to help sb –
13 **to retain** to keep – 17 **to confine sb** to stop sb from leaving a place – 17 **Oyster Card**
an electronic ticket for public transport in and around London, which is topped up with
money – 24 **premises** *(pl)* the buildings and land owned by sb

and thankful for the semi-darkness in which the health club, for some reason, kept its clientele, as if the place were a night club, or a midnight Mass. The darkness helped disguise the fact that her swimming costume was in fact a sturdy black bra
5 and a pair of plain black cotton knickers. No, on balance she did not think she was a slave.

0–8

The woman exiting the Embassy of Cambodia did not look especially like a New Person or an Old Person – neither clearly
10 of the city nor of the country – and of course it is a long time since this division meant anything in Cambodia. Nor did these terms mean anything to Fatou, who was curious only to catch her first sighting of a possible Cambodian anywhere near the Embassy of Cambodia. She was particularly interested in the
15 woman's clothes, which were precise and utilitarian – a gray shirt tucked tightly into a pair of tan slacks, a blue mackintosh, a droopy rain hat – just as if she were a man, or no different from a man. Her straight black hair was cut short. She had in her hands many bags from Sainsbury's, and this Fatou found
20 a little mysterious: where was she taking all that shopping? It also surprised her that the woman from the Embassy of Cambodia should shop in the same Willesden branch of Sainsbury's where Fatou shopped for the Derawals. She had an idea that Oriental people had their own, secret establish-
25 ments. (She believed the Jews did, too.) She both admired and slightly resented this self-reliance, but had no doubt that it was the secret to holding great power, as a people. For example,

---

4 **sturdy** robust, giving good support – 5 **knickers** *(BE)* underpants, panties – 9 **New Person / Old Person** New People were mainly from urban areas and forced to work in terrible conditions under the Khmer Rouge. People from rural areas were called Old People by the regime. – 15 **utilitarian** functional, practical – 16 **tan slacks** light brown pants – 16 **mackintosh** *(BE, old)* raincoat – 19 **Sainsbury's** a large British supermarket chain – 24 **establishment** *here:* business – 26 **to resent** to dislike, to be bitter about

when the Chinese had come to Fatou's village to take over the mine, an abiding local mystery had been: what did they eat and where did they eat it? They certainly did not buy food in the market, or from the Lebanese traders along the main road.
5 They made their own arrangements. (Whether back home or here, the key to surviving as a people, in Fatou's opinion, was to make your own arrangements.)

But, looking again at the bags the Cambodian woman carried, Fatou wondered whether they weren't in fact very old
10 bags – hadn't their design changed? The more she looked at them the more convinced she became that they contained not food but clothes or something else again, the outline of each bag being a little too rounded and smooth. Maybe she was simply taking out the rubbish. Fatou stood at the bus stop and
15 watched until the Cambodian woman reached the corner, crossed, and turned left toward the high road. Meanwhile, back at the embassy the badminton continued to be played, though with a little more effort now because of a wayward wind. At one point it seemed to Fatou that the next lob would
20 blow southward, sending the shuttlecock over the wall to land lightly in her own hands. Instead the other player, with his vicious reliability (Fatou had long ago decided that both players were men), caught the shuttlecock as it began to drift and sent it back to his opponent – another deathly, downward
25 smash.

0–9

No doubt there are those who will be critical of the narrow, essentially local scope of Fatou's interest in the Cambodian woman from the Embassy of Cambodia, but we, the people
30 of Willesden, have some sympathy with her attitude. The fact

---

2 **abiding** lasting, enduring – 18 **wayward** unmanageable, unpredictable – 28 **scope** range

is if we followed the history of every little country in this world – in its dramatic as well as its quiet times – we would have no space left in which to live our own lives or to apply ourselves to our necessary tasks, never mind indulge in occasional
5 pleasures, like swimming. Surely there is something to be said for drawing a circle around our attention and remaining within that circle. But how large should this circle be?

0–10

It was the Sunday after Fatou saw the Cambodian that she
10 decided to put a version of this question to Andrew, as they sat in the Tunisian café eating two large fingers of dough stuffed with cream and custard and topped with a strip of chocolate icing. Specifically, she began a conversation with Andrew about the Holocaust, as Andrew was the only person
15 she had found in London with whom she could have these deep conversations, partly because he was patient and sympathetic to her, but also because he was an educated person, currently studying for a part-time business degree at the College of North West London. With his student card he
20 had been given free, twenty-four-hour access to the Internet.
  "But more people died in Rwanda," Fatou argued. "And nobody speaks about that! Nobody!"
  "Yes, I think that's true," Andrew conceded, and put the first of four sugars in his coffee. "I have to check. But, yes, millions
25 and millions. They hide the true numbers, but you can see them online. There's always a lot of hiding; it's the same all over. It's like this bureaucratic Nigerian government – they are the greatest at numerology, hiding figures, changing them to

---

11 **dough** a raw or baked mixture of ingredients, which makes up the basis of cake or biscuits – 12 **custard** a sweet yellow sauce eaten with desserts – 21 **Rwanda** reference to the Rwanda genocide of 1994. The exact number of dead is not known, but it is estimated that ~1 million people were killed of a total population of ~7.5 million – 23 **to concede sth** to admit that sth is true

suit their purposes. I have a name for it: I call it 'demonology.' Not 'numerology' – 'demonology.' "

"Yes, but what I am saying is like this," Fatou pressed, wary of the conversation's drifting back, as it usually did, to the
5 financial corruption of the Nigerian government. "Are we born to suffer? Sometimes I think we were born to suffer more than all the rest."

Andrew pushed his professorial glasses up his nose. "But, Fatou, you're forgetting the most important thing. Who cried
10 most for Jesus? His mother. Who cries most for you? Your father. It's very logical, when you break it down. The Jews cry for the Jews. The Russians cry for the Russians. We cry for Africa, because we are Africans, and, even then, I'm sorry, Fatou" – Andrew's chubby face creased up in a smile – "if
15 Nigeria plays Ivory Coast and we beat you into the ground, I'm laughing, man! I can't lie. I'm celebrating. Stomp! Stomp!" He did a little dance with his upper body, and Fatou tried, not for the first time, to imagine what he might be like as a husband, but could see only herself as the wife, and Andrew
20 as a teenage son of hers, bright and helpful, to be sure, but a son all the same – though in reality he was three years older than she. Surely it was wrong to find his baby fat and struggling moustache so off-putting. Here was a good man! She knew that he cared for her, was clean, and had given his life to Christ.
25 Still, some part of her rebelled against him, some unholy part.

"Hush your mouth," she said, trying to sound more playful than disgusted, and was relieved when he stopped jiggling and laid both his hands on the table, his face suddenly quite solemn.

---

1 **demonology** an invented word in this sense that combines the meanings 'harmful', 'deceitful' and 'skilful' of the word 'demon' (all characteristics of a demon); an allusion to the widespread corruption in Nigerian government, legal and financial institutions – 3 **wary** cautious – 14 **chubby** round, plump – 27 **to jiggle** to move quickly up and down or from side to side; to shake – 29 **solemn** serious

"Believe me, that's a natural law, Fatou, pure and simple. Only God cries for us all, because we are all his children. It's very, very logical. You just have to think about it for a moment."

Fatou sighed, and spooned some coffee foam into her
5   mouth. "But I still think we have more pain. I've seen it myself. Chinese people have never been slaves. They are always protected from the worst."

Andrew took off his glasses and rubbed them on the end of his shirt. Fatou could tell that he was preparing to lay
10   knowledge upon her.

"Fatou, think about it for a moment, please: what about Hiroshima?"

It was a name Fatou had heard before, but sometimes Andrew's superior knowledge made her nervous. She would
15   find herself struggling to remember even the things she had believed she already knew.

"The big wave . . ." she began, uncertainly – it was the wrong answer. He laughed mightily and shook his head at her.

"No, man! Big bomb. Biggest bomb in the world, made by
20   the U.S.A., of course. They killed five million people in one second. Can you imagine that? You think just because your eyes are like this" – he tugged the skin at both temples – "you're always protected? Think again. This bomb, even if it didn't blow you up, a week later it melted the skin off your bones."

25   Fatou realized that she had heard this story before, or some version of it. But she felt the same vague impatience with it as she did with all accounts of suffering in the distant past. For what could be done about the suffering of the past?

"O.K.," she said. "Maybe all people have their hard times, in
30   the past of history, but I still say –"

"Here is a counterpoint," Andrew said, reaching out and gripping her shoulder. "Let me ask you, Fatou, seriously, think

---

12 **Hiroshima** city in Japan, onto which the USA dropped an atomic bomb in August 1945 – 22 **temple** an area on each side of the face between one's ear and one's forehead *(Schläfe)*

about this. I'm sorry to interrupt you, but I have thought a lot about this and I want to pass it on to you, because I know you care about things seriously, not like these people." He waved a hand at the assortment of cake eaters at other tables. "You're 5 not like the other girls I know, just thinking about the club and their hair. You're a person who thinks. I told you before, anything you want to know about, ask me – I'll look it up, I'll do the research. I have access. Then I'll bring it to you."

"You're a very good friend to me, Andrew, I know that."

10 "Listen, we are friends to each other. In this world you need friends. But, Fatou, listen to my question. It's a counterpoint to what you have been saying. Tell me, why would God choose us especially for suffering when we, above all others, praise his name? Africa is the fastest-growing Christian continent! 15 Just think about it for a minute! It doesn't even make sense!"

"But it's not him," Fatou said quietly, looking over Andrew's shoulder at the rain beating on the window. "It's the Devil."

0–11

Andrew and Fatou sat in the Tunisian coffee shop, waiting for 20 it to stop raining, but it did not stop raining, and at 3 P.M. Fatou said she would just have to get wet. She shared Andrew's umbrella as far as the Overground, letting him pull her into his clammy, high-smelling body as they walked. At Brondesbury station Andrew had to get the train, and so they said goodbye. 25 Several times he tried to press his umbrella on her, but Fatou knew the walk from Acton Central to Andrew's bed-sit was long and she refused to let him suffer on her account.

"Big woman. Won't let anybody protect you."

"Rain doesn't scare me."

---

4 **assortment** mix, variety – 11 **counterpoint** *here:* contrast – 23 **clammy** slightly wet, damp in an unpleasant way – 26 **bed-sit** a form of accommodation consisting of a single room and a place to cook, and access to a shared bathroom

Fatou took from her pocket a swimming cap she had found on the floor of the health-club changing room. She wound her plaits into a bun and pulled the cap over her head.

"That's a very original idea," Andrew said, laughing. "You
5 should market that! Make your first million!"

"Peace be with you," Fatou said, and kissed him chastely on the cheek. Andrew did the same, lingering a little longer with his kiss than was necessary.

0–12

10 By the time Fatou reached the Derawals', only her hair was dry, but before going to get changed she rushed to the kitchen to take the lamb out of the freezer, though it was pointless – there were not enough hours before dinner – and then upstairs to collect the dirty clothes from the matching wicker baskets
15 in four different bedrooms. There was no one in the master bedroom, or in Faizul's, or Julie's. Downstairs a television was blaring. Entering Asma's room, hearing nothing, assuming it empty, Fatou headed straight for the laundry bin in the corner. As she opened the lid she felt a hand hit her hard on the back;
20 she turned around.

There was the youngest, Asma, in front of her, her mouth open like a trout fish. Before Fatou could understand, Asma punched the huge pile of clothes out of her hands. Fatou stooped to retrieve them. While she was kneeling on the floor,
25 another strike came, a kick to her arm. She left the clothes where they were and got up, frightened by her own anger. But when she looked at Asma now she saw the girl gesturing frantically at her own throat, then putting her hands together in prayer, and then back to her throat once more. Her eyes

---

3 **plait** [plæt] braid, a way of combining three lengths of hair in a special pattern (*Zopf*) – 6 **chastely** in an innocent way – 14 **wicker basket** a basket made of thin pieces of wood woven together – 24 **to stoop** to bend down

were bulging. She veered suddenly to the right; she threw herself over the back of a chair. When she turned back to Fatou her face was gray and Fatou understood finally and ran to her, grabbed her round her waist, and pulled upward as she had been taught in the hotel. A marble – with an iridescent ribbon of blue at its centre, like a wave – flew from the child's mouth and landed wetly in the carpet's plush.

Asma wept and drew in frantic gulps of air. Fatou gave her a hug, and worried when the clothes would get done. Together they went down to the den, where the rest of the family was watching "Britain's Got Talent" on a flat-screen TV attached to the wall. Everybody stood at the sight of Asma's wild weeping. Mr Derawal paused the Sky box. Fatou explained about the marble.

"How many times I tell you not to put things in your mouth?" Mr Derawal asked, and Mrs Derawal said something in their language – Fatou heard the name of their God – and pulled Asma onto the sofa and stroked her daughter's silky black hair.

"I couldn't breathe, man! I couldn't call nobody," Asma cried. "I was gonna die!"

"What you putting marbles in your mouth for anyway, you idiot," Faizul said, and un-paused the Sky box. "What kind of chief puts a marble in her mouth? Idiot. Bet you was bricking it."

"Oi, she saved your life," said Julie, the eldest child, whom Fatou generally liked the least. "Fatou saved your life. That's deep."

"I woulda just done this," Faizul said, and performed an especially dramatic Heimlich to his own skinny body. "And if that didn't work I woulda just start pounding myself karate style, bam bam bam bam bam – "

---

1 **to bulge** to stick out, to protrude – 5 **iridescent** having bright colours which seem to change – 10 **den** a room used for free time activities – 23 **to brick it** *(sl, vulg)* to be very scared – 29 **Heimlich** Heimlich manoeuvre, a technique to remove an object trapped in a person's throat which prevents them from breathing

"Faizul!" Mr Derawal shouted, and then turned stiffly to Fatou, and spoke not to her, exactly, but to a point somewhere between her elbow and the sunburst mirror behind her head. "Thank you, Fatou. It's lucky you were there."

5 Fatou nodded and moved to leave, but at the doorway to the den Mrs Derawal asked her if the lamb had defrosted and Fatou had to confess that she had only just taken it out. Mrs Derawal said something sharply in her language. Fatou waited for something further, but Mr Derawal only smiled awkwardly 10 at her, and nodded as a sign that she could go now. Fatou went upstairs to collect the clothes.

0–13

"To keep you is no benefit. To destroy you is no loss" was one of the mottoes of the Khmer Rouge. It referred to the New 15 People, those city dwellers who could not be made to give up city life and work on a farm. By returning everybody to the land, the regime hoped to create a society of Old People – that is to say, of agrarian peasants. When a New Person was relocated from the city to the country, it was vital not to show 20 weakness in the fields. Vulnerability was punishable by death.

In Willesden, we are almost all New People, though some of us, like Fatou, were, until quite recently, Old People, working the land in our various countries of origin. Of the Old and New People of Willesden I speak; I have been chosen to speak for 25 them, though they did not choose me and must wonder what gives me the right. I could say, "Because I was born at the crossroads of Willesden, Kilburn, and Queen's Park!" But the reply would be swift and damning: "Oh, don't be foolish, many

---

14 **Khmer Rouge** Cambodian Communist party responsible for the genocide in Cambodia between 1975 and 1979. The party's aim was to forcefully turn Cambodia into a socialist agrarian republic. – 18 **peasant** a person working on a farm, generally poor and of low social status – 20 **vulnerability** weakness, sensitivity – 28 **swift** quick

people were born right there; it doesn't mean anything at all. We are not one people and no one can speak for us. It's all a lot of nonsense. We see you standing on the balcony, overlooking the Embassy of Cambodia, in your dressing gown,
5 staring into the chestnut trees, looking gormless. The real reason you speak in this way is because you can't think of anything better to do."

0–14

On Monday, Fatou went swimming. She paused to watch the
10 badminton. She thought that the arm that delivered the smashes must make a movement similar to the one she made in the pool, with her clumsy yet effective front crawl. She entered the health centre and gave a guest pass to the girl behind the desk. In the dimly lit changing room, she put on
15 her sturdy black underwear. As she swam, she thought of Carib Beach. Her father serving snapper to the guests on the deck, his bow tie always a little askew, the ugly tourists, the whole scene there. Of course, it was not surprising in the least to see old white men from Germany with beautiful local girls on their
20 laps, but she would never forget the two old white women from England – red women, really, thanks to the sun – each of them as big as two women put together, with Kweku and Osai lying by their sides, the boys hooking their scrawny black bird-arms round the women's massive red shoulders, dancing
25 with them in the hotel "ballroom," answering to the names Michael and David, and disappearing into the women's cabins at night. She had known the boys' real girlfriends; they were chambermaids like Fatou. Sometimes they cleaned the rooms where Kweku and Osai spent the night with the English

---

5 **gormless** stupid, slow to understand – 16 **snapper** a type of fish – 17 **bow tie** a piece of clothing for men which is tied around their neck in the shape of a bow *(Fliege)* – 17 **askew** *opp of* straight

women. And the girls themselves had "boyfriends" among the guests. It was not a holy place, that hotel. And the pool was shaped like a kidney bean: nobody could really swim in it, or showed any sign of wanting to. Mostly, they stood in it and
5 drank cocktails. Sometimes they even had their burgers delivered to the pool. Fatou hated to watch her father crouching to hand a burger to a man waist high in water.

The only good thing that happened in Carib Beach was this: once a month, on a Sunday, the congregation of a local church
10 poured out of a coach at the front gates, lined up fully dressed in the courtyard, and then walked into the pool for a mass baptism. The tourists were never warned, and Fatou never understood why the congregants were allowed to do it. But she loved to watch their white shirts bloat and spread across
15 the surface of the water, and to hear the weeping and singing. At the time – though she was not then a member of that church, or of any church except the one in her heart – she had felt that this baptism was for her, too, and that it kept her safe, and that this was somehow the reason she did not become
20 one of the "girls" at the Carib Beach Resort. For almost two years – between her father's efforts and the grace of an unseen and unacknowledged God – she did her work, and swam Sunday mornings at the crack of dawn, and got along all right. But the Devil was waiting.
25 She had only a month left in Accra when she entered a bedroom to clean it one morning and heard the door shut softly behind her before she could put a hand to it. He came, this time, in Russian form. Afterward, he cried and begged her not to tell anyone: his wife had gone to see the Cape Coast
30 Castle and they were leaving the following morning. Fatou listened to his blubbering and realized that he thought the

---

7 **to crouch** to bend your legs and lean forward – 9 **congregation** people attending a church service; the parish of a church – 12 **baptism** christening, the act of making a person a member of a church and giving them their name *(Taufe)* – 31 **blubbering** weeping, noisy crying

hotel would punish him for his action, or that the police would be called. That was when she knew that the Devil was stupid as well as evil. She spat in his face and left. Thinking about the Devil now made her swimming fast and angry, and for a
5   while she easily lapped the young white man in the lane next to hers, the faster lane.

0–15

"Don't give the Devil your anger, it is his food," Andrew had said to her, when they first met, a year ago. He handed her a
10 leaflet as she sat eating a sandwich on a bench in Kilburn Park. "Don't make it so easy for him." Without being invited, he took the seat next to hers and began going through the text of his leaflet. It was printed to look like a newspaper, and he started with the headline: "WHY IS THERE PAIN?" She liked him. They
15 began a theological conversation. It continued in the Tunisian café, and every Sunday for several months. A lot of the things he said she had heard before from other people, and they did not succeed in changing her attitude. In the end, it was one thing that he said to her that really made the difference. It was
20 after she'd told him this story:
      "One day, at the hotel, I heard a commotion on the beach. It was early morning. I went out and I saw nine children washed up dead on the beach. Ten or eleven years old, boys and girls. They had gone into the water, but they didn't
25 know how to swim. Some people were crying, maybe two people. Everyone else just shook their heads and carried on walking to where they were going. After a long time, the police came. The bodies were taken away. People said, 'Well, they are with God now.' Everybody carried on like before. I went back
30 to work. The next year I arrived in Rome. I saw a boy who

---

5 **to lap** to overtake sb who is still on an earlier lap *(überrunden)* – 21 **commotion** noisy disorder, confusion

was about fifteen years old knocked down on his bike. He was dead. People were screaming and crying in the street. Everybody crying. They were not his family. They were only strangers. The next day, it was in the paper."

5 And Andrew replied, "A tap runs fast the first time you switch it on."

0–16

Twenty more laps. Fatou tried to think of the last time she had cried. It was in Rome, but it wasn't for the boy on the bike.

10 She was cleaning toilets in a Catholic girls' school. She did not know Jesus then, so it made no difference what kind of school it was – she knew only that she was cleaning toilets. At midday, she had a fifteen-minute break. She would go to the little walled garden across the road to smoke a cigarette. One day,

15 she was sitting on a bench near a fountain, and spotted something odd in the bushes. A tin of green paint. A gold spray can. A Statue of Liberty costume. An identity card with the name Rajib Devanga. One shoe. An empty wallet. A plastic tub with a slit cut in the top meant for coins and euro notes –

20 empty. A little stain of what looked like blood on this tub. Until that point, she had been envious of the Bengali boys on Via Nazionale. She felt that she, too, could paint herself green and stand still for an hour. But when she tried to find out more the Bengalis would not talk to her. It was a closed shop, for

25 brown men only. Her place was in the bathroom stalls. She thought those men had it easy. Then she saw that little sad pile of belongings in the bush and cried; for herself or for Rajib, she wasn't sure.

Now she turned onto her back in the water for the final two

30 laps, relaxed her arms, and kicked her feet out like a frog. Water

---

5 **tap** *(BE)* a device which can be opened or closed to control how much liquid or gas is released from a pipe, e.g. on a sink

made her think of more water. "When you're baptized in our church, all sin is wiped, you start again": Andrew's promise. She had never told Andrew of the sin precisely, but she knew that he knew she was not a virgin. The day she finally became a Catholic, February 6, 2011, Andrew had taken her, hair still wet, to the Tunisian café and asked her how it felt.

She was joyful! She said, "I feel like a new person!"

But happiness like that is hard to hold on to. Back at work the next day, picking Julie's dirty underwear up off the floor inches from the wicker basket, she had to keep reminding herself of her new relationship with Jesus and how it changed everything. Didn't it change everything? The following Sunday she expressed some of her doubt, cautiously, to Andrew.

"But did you think you'd never feel sad again? Never angry or tired or just pissed off – sorry about my language. Come on, Fatou! Wise up, man!"

Was it wrong to hope to be happy?

0–17

Lost to these watery thoughts, Fatou got home a little later than usual and was through the door only minutes before Mrs Derawal.

"How is Asma?" Fatou asked. She had heard the girl cry out in the night.

"My goodness, it was just a little marble," Mrs Derawal said, and Fatou realized that it was not in her imagination: since Sunday night, neither of the adult Derawals had been able to look her in the eye. "What a fuss everybody is making. I have a list for you – it's on the table."

---

15 **pissed off** *(sl, vulg)* annoyed – 27 **fuss** unnecessary worry or excitement

0–18

Fatou watched Andrew pick his way through the tables in the Tunisian café, holding a tray with a pair of mochas on it and some croissants. He hit the elbow of one man with his backside
5 and then trailed the belt of his long, silly leather coat through the lunch of another, apologizing as he went. You could not say that he was an elegant man. But he was generous, he was thoughtful. She stood up to push a teetering croissant back onto its plate. They sat down at the same time, and smiled at
10 each other.

"A while ago you asked me about Cambodia," Andrew said. "Well, it's a very interesting case." He tapped the frame of his glasses. "If you even wore a pair of these? They would kill you. Glasses meant you thought too much. They had very primitive
15 ideas. They were enemies of logic and progress. They wanted everybody to go back to the country and live like simple people."

"But sometimes it's true that things are simpler in the country."

20 "In some ways. I don't really know. I've never lived in the country."

I don't really know. It was good to hear him say that! It was a good sign. She smiled cheekily at him. "People are less sinful in the country," she said, but he did not seem to see that she
25 was flirting with him, and embarked on another lecture:

"That's true. But you can't force people to live in the country. That's what I call a Big Man Policy. I invented this phrase for my dissertation. We know all about Big Man Policies in Nigeria. They come from the top, and they crush you. There's always
30 somebody who wants to be the Big Man, and take everything for himself, and tell everybody how to think and what to do.

---

8 **teetering** about to fall off – 23 **cheekily** in a bold, slightly disrespectful but playful way – 25 **to embark on sth** to start sth

When, actually, it's he who is weak. But if the Big Men see that you see that they are weak they have no choice but to destroy you. That is the real tragedy."

Fatou sighed. "I never met a man who didn't want to tell
5 everybody how to think and what to do," she said.

Andrew laughed. "Fatou, you include me? Are you a feminist now, too?"

Fatou brought her mug up to her lips and looked penetratingly at Andrew. There were good and bad kinds of weakness
10 in men, and she had come to the conclusion that the key was to know which kind you were dealing with.

"Andrew," she said, putting her hand on his, "would you like to come swimming with me?"

0–19

15 Because Fatou believed that the Derawals' neighbours had been instructed to spy on her, she would not let Andrew come to the house to pick her up on Monday, instead leaving as she always did, just before ten, carrying misleading Sainsbury's bags and walking toward the health centre. She spotted him
20 from a long way off – the road was so straight and he had arrived early. He stood shivering in the drizzle. She felt sorry, but also a little prideful: it was the prospect of seeing her body that had raised this big man from his bed. Still, it was a sacrifice, she knew, for her friend to come out to meet her on
25 a weekday morning. He worked all night long and kept the daytime for sleeping. She watched him waving at her from their agreed meeting spot, just on the corner, in front of the Embassy of Cambodia. After a while, he stopped waving – because she was still so far away – and then, a little later, he

---

8 **mug** a big cup – 8 **penetratingly** in a way that makes a person think that one is looking right into them – 21 **drizzle** light rain

began waving again. She waved back, and when she finally reached him they surprised each other by holding hands. "I'm an excellent badminton player," Andrew said, as they passed the Embassy of Cambodia. "I would make you weep for mercy!
5 Next time, instead of swimming we should play badminton somewhere." Next time, we should go to Paris. Next time, we should go to the moon. He was a dreamer. But there are worse things, Fatou thought, than being a dreamer.

0–20

10 "So you're a guest and this is your guest?" the girl behind the desk asked.

"I am a guest and this is another guest," Fatou replied.

"Yeah . . . that's not really how it works?"

"Please," Fatou said. "We've come from a long way."

15 "I appreciate that," the girl said. "But I really shouldn't let you in, to be honest."

"Please," Fatou said again. She could think of no other argument.

The girl took out a pen and made a mark on Fatou's guest
20 pass.

"This one time. Don't tell no one I did this, please. One time only! I'll need to cross off two separate visits."

For one time only, then, Andrew and Fatou approached the changing rooms together and parted at the doors that led to
25 the men's and the women's. In her changing room, Fatou got ready with lightning speed. Yet somehow he was already there on a lounger when she came out, eyes trained on the women's changing-room door, waiting for her to emerge.

"Man, this is the life!" he said, putting his arms behind his
30 head.

27 **lounger** a comfortable chair to sit or lie on

"Are you getting in?" Fatou asked, and tried to place her hands, casually, in front of her groin.

"Not yet, man, I'm just taking it all in, taking it all in. You go in. I'll come in a moment."

5　Fatou climbed down the steps and began to swim. Not elegant, not especially fast, but consistent and determined. Every now and then she would angle her head to try to see if Andrew was still on his chair, smiling to himself. After twenty laps, she swam to where he lay and put her elbows on the
10　tiles.

"You're not coming in? It's so warm. Like a bath."

"Sure, sure," he said. "I'll try it."

As he sat up his stomach folded in on itself, and Fatou wondered whether he had spent all that time on the lounger
15　to avoid her seeing its precise bulk and wobble. He came toward the stairs; Fatou held out a hand to him, but he pushed it away. He made his way down and stood in the shallow end, splashing water over his shoulders like a prince fanning himself, and then crouching down into it.

20　"It is warm! Very nice. This is the life, man! You go, swim – I'll follow you."

Fatou kicked off, creating so much splash that she heard someone in the adjacent lane complain. At the wall, she turned and looked for Andrew. His method, such as it was, involved
25　dipping deep under the water and hanging there like a hippo, then batting his arms till he crested for air, and then diving down again and hanging. It was a lot of energy to expend on such a short distance, and by the time he reached the wall he was panting like a maniac. His eyes – he had no goggles – were
30　painfully red.

---

2 **groin** front part of one's body between one's legs – 10 **tile** a thin usually square or rectangular piece of baked clay or other substances used to cover the floor or the walls *(Kachel, Fliese)* – 23 **adjacent** next – 29 **to pant** to breathe loudly and fast, to gasp for air

"It's O.K.," Fatou said, trying to take his hand again. "If you let me, I'll show you how." But he shrugged her off, and rubbed at his eyes.

"There's too much bloody chlorine in this pool."

5   "You want to leave?"

Andrew turned back to look at Fatou. His eyes were streaming. He looked, to Fatou, like a little boy trying to disguise the fact he had been crying. But then he held her hand, under the water.

10   "No. I'm just going to take it easy right here."

"O.K.," Fatou said.

"You swim. You're good. You swim."

"O.K.," Fatou said, and set off, and found that each lap was more distracted and rhythmless than the last. She was not
15 used to being watched while she swam. Ten laps later, she suddenly stood up halfway down the lane and walked the rest of the distance to the wall.

"You want to go in the Jacuzzi?" she asked him, pointing to it. In the hot tub sat a woman dressed in a soaking tracksuit,
20 her head covered with a head scarf. A man next to the woman, perhaps her husband, stared at Fatou and said something to her. He was so hairy he was almost as covered as she was. Together they rose up out of the water and left. He was wearing the tiniest of Speedos, the kind Fatou had feared Andrew might
25 wear, and was grateful he had not. Andrew's shorts were perfectly nice, knee-length, red and solid, and looked good against his skin.

"No," Andrew said. "It's great just to be here with you, watching the world go by."

---

14 **distracted** unable to concentrate on sth – 19 **tracksuit** comfortable trousers and top usually worn for sports or for relaxing

0–21

That same evening, Fatou was fired. Not for the guest passes – the Derawals never found out how many miles Fatou had travelled on their membership. In fact, it was hard for Fatou
5 to understand exactly why she was being fired, as Mrs Derawal herself did not seem able to explain it very precisely.

"What you don't understand is that we have no need for a nanny," she said, standing in the doorway of Fatou's room – there was not really enough space in there for two people to stand
10 without one of them being practically on the bed. "The children are grown. We need a housekeeper, one who cleans properly. These days, you care more about the children than the cleaning," Mrs Derawal added, though Fatou had never cared for the children, not even slightly. "And that is of no use to us."

15 Fatou said nothing. She was thinking that she did not have a proper suitcase and would have to take her things from Mrs Derawal's house in plastic bags.

"And so you will want to find somewhere else to live as soon as possible," Mrs Derawal said. "My husband's cousin is
20 coming to stay in this room on Friday – this Friday."

Fatou thought about that for a moment. Then she said, "Can I please use the phone for one call?"

Mrs Derawal inspected a piece of wood that had flaked from the doorframe. But she nodded.

25 "And I would like to have my passport, please."

"Excuse me?"

"My passport, please."

At last Mrs Derawal looked at Fatou, right into her eyes, but her face was twisted, as if Fatou had just reached over and
30 slapped her. Anyone could see the Devil had climbed inside poor Mrs Derawal. He was lighting her up with a pure fury.

"For goodness' sake, girl, I don't have your passport! What would I want with your passport? It's probably in a drawer in the kitchen somewhere. Is that my job now, too, to look for
35 your things?"

Fatou was left alone. She packed her things into the decoy shopping bags she usually took to the swimming pool. While she was doing this, someone pushed her passport under the door. An hour later, she carried her bags downstairs and went
5 directly to the phone in the hall. Faizul walked by and lifted his hand for a high-five. Fatou ignored him and dialled Andrew's number. From her friend's voice she knew that she had woken him, but he was not even the slightest bit angry. He listened to all she had to say and seemed to understand,
10 too, without her having to say so, that at this moment she could not speak freely. After she had said her part, he asked a few quick technical questions and then explained clearly and carefully what was to happen.

"It will all be O.K. They need cleaners in my offices – I will
15 ask for you. In the meantime, you come here. We'll sleep in shifts. You can trust me. I respect you, Fatou."

But she did not have her Oyster Card; it was in the kitchen, on the fridge under a magnet of Florida, and she would rather die than go in there. Fine: he could meet her at 6 P.M., at the
20 Brondesbury Overground station. Fatou looked at the grand-father clock in front of her: she had four hours to kill.

"Six o' clock," she repeated. She put the phone down, took the rest of the guest passes from the drawer of the Louis XVI console, and left the house.

25 "Weighed down a bit today," the girl at the desk of the health club said, nodding at Fatou's collection of plastic bags. Fatou held out a guest pass for a stamp and did not smile. "See you next time," this same girl said, an hour and a half later, as Fatou strode past, still weighed down and still unwilling to be
30 grateful for past favours. Gratitude was just another kind of servitude. Better to make your own arrangements.

---

1 **decoy** sth used to trick or deceive people – 31 **servitude** enslavement

Walking out into the cold grey, Fatou felt a sense of brightness, of being washed clean, that neither the weather nor her new circumstance could dim. Still, her limbs were weary and her hair was wet; she would probably catch a cold,
5   waiting out here. It was only four-thirty. She put her bags on the pavement and sat down next to them, just by the bus stop opposite the Embassy of Cambodia. Buses came and went, slowing down for her and then jerking forward when they realized that she had no interest in getting up and on. Many
10 of us walked past her that afternoon, or spotted her as we rode the bus, or through the windscreens of our cars, or from our balconies. Naturally, we wondered what this girl was doing, sitting on the damp pavement in the middle of the day. We worried for her. We tend to assume the worst, here in Willesden.
15 We watched her watching the shuttlecock. Pock, smash. Pock, smash. As if one player could imagine only a violent conclusion and the other only a hopeful return.